Stan Won't Dance

presents

Babel

babel. *noun*. a confused noise made by a number of voices.

Written by Patrick Neate

Directed by Liam Steel and Rob Tannion

D1341619

BABEL was first performed at Laban Theatre, London,
21 January 2010 with the following company:

Direction Liam Steel & Rob Tannion
Choreography Liam Steel & Rob Tannion in collaboration
  with the performers
Text Patrick Neate
Performers Nathaniel Parchment, Moreno Solinas, Hugh
  Stanier, Dan Watson, Matthew Winston

Design Liam Steel
Lighting Design Andy Purves
Sound Design Gareth Fry
Video Design Matt Spencer
Executive Director Ellie Beedham
Production Manager Jon Woodley
Technical Stage Manager Andy Guard
Sound Technician Chris Reid
Marketing Tiffany Evans
Administration & Education Hanna Streeter
General Management Dan Projects
Advisors Bridget Thornborrow, Steve Manix, Heather Green

Thanks to: Marie McCluskey; Deryck Newland; Brian Brady;
  Lisa Mead; Kenny Baraka; The Jerwood Space; The Place;
  James Hogan at Oberon Books.

BABEL was commissioned by Swindon Dance and Salisbury
Arts Centre, co-produced by Laban Theatre and Stan Won't
Dance in association with Apples and Snakes, supported by
Arts Council England and the Esmée Fairbairn Foundation.

STAN WON'T DANCE

Stan Won't Dance was formed in December 2003 by Ellie Beedham, Liam Steel and Rob Tannion, out of a shared vision to expand the boundaries of Dance and Physical Theatre.

The company collaborates with writers or uses existing script to seamlessly combine spoken word and choreography - producing significant and profound 'dance-theatre' out of unexpected tales and dangerous texts. Side stepping the idea that only a niche audience can enjoy dance, the company places real people in real situations at the heart of the work. Engaging audiences in as many ways as possible - emotionally, physically, psychologically and intellectually - the aim is to create brutally honest, challenging and inspiring work that is accessible to all.

By removing the safety net of expected dance parameters, Stan Won't Dance has committed itself to making work that shatters traditional conventions and expectations. Collaborating with fellow artists and inviting them to work with us in new and potentially demanding ways, the company utilises and combines other performance disciplines to push at the edges of the dance-theatre definition, and discover an innovative and distinct theatrical voice.

Stan Won't Dance firmly believes that a dance performance has the ability to raise fundamental questions and should be an arena of debate and danger as well as artistry and entertainment. As such, with each new project, the company is striving to excite and invigorate audiences with work that is fresh, exigent, imaginative, potent, and popular without having to be populist, and makes a significant contribution to this country's cultural development – both artistic and societal.

2003

STAN WON'T DANCE formed by Ellie Beedham, Rob Tannion & Liam Steel.

2004

SINNER

Original idea & text by Ben Payne
Directed and choreographed by Rob Tannion & Liam Steel

Co-produced by Southbank Centre and Stan Won't Dance in association with Laban. Co-commissioned by South Hill Park, Bracknell, Corn Exchange, Newbury and Swindon Dance. Supported by the European Union Culture 2000 Programme, Arts Council England, The British Council and The Junction, Cambridge.

World première 7 May 2004 Purcell Room, Southbank Centre, London.

Developed into full-length piece. National tour of UK.

2006

Sinner tour of USA and Canada and second tour of UK.

Nominated for Canadian DORA Award and GLAAD Media Award.

REVELATIONS

Conceived & directed by Liam Steel
Choreographed by Rob Tannion & Liam Steel
Text by Nigel Charnock

Co-produced by Southbank Centre and Stan Won't Dance in association with Laban. Commissioned and presented by Dance Touring Partnership and supported by Arts Council England, the Esmée Fairbairn Foundation and the Jerwood Charitable Foundation. *Revelations* was developed through

Jerwood Changing Stages Choreolab 2 at DanceXchange and at The Lowry, Salford as part of its Choreographers in Residence scheme.

World première 12 October 2006 Laban Theatre, London, followed by UK tour.

2007

SKYLON SPIRITS

A series of aerial bungee duets on the masts outside the Royal Festival Hall.

Commissioned by Southbank Centre to celebrate the re-opening of the Royal Festival Hall.

OFF THE WALL

Directed and choreographed by Rob Tannion & Liam Steel
Based on E.M. Forster's *The Machine Stops*

A large outdoor spectacular with over a hundred artists performing on the walls and rooftops of the Southbank Centre, London.

Commissioned by Southbank Centre. Co-produced by Southbank Centre and Stan Won't Dance in association with Laban, The Circus Space and London College of Fashion.

www.stanwontdance.com

Join the e-list to receive news about future projects and tours. You can also find us on Facebook and Twitter.

Liam Steel Director/Designer/Choreographer

Committed to defining new theatrical languages, Liam has gained an international reputation as being one of Britain's leading physical theatre practitioners. He has directed, choreographed or performed with all of the most influential companies in this country, including Complicité, Volcano Theatre Company, Nigel Charnock & Company and David Glass Ensemble. Before Stan Won't Dance, he was probably most widely recognised for his work with Frantic Assembly, with whom he has created four productions, and with DV8 Physical Theatre, where he was a core member for eight years, working as a performer, assistant director and designer. During his time with DV8 he worked on five international tours and the Emmy award-winning film version of *Enter Achilles*.

Liam also has extensive experience as a director and choreographer in the repertory sector. His experience includes work with the Royal National Theatre, Regents Park Open Air Theatre, Nottingham Playhouse, Birmingham Rep, Northampton Theatre Royal, The Royal Court, Manchester Royal Exchange, The RSC, and five productions at the Library Theatre, Manchester. In addition his work has spanned West End musical theatre, opera, contemporary dance commissions and international new circus. The summer of 2009 saw him stage the theatrical extravaganza *Ben Hur* for the O2 arena and stadiums worldwide with a cast of over 300 performers and 46 horses!

His awards include: TMA Award for Best Production for Young People for *Tom's Midnight Garden* at the Library Theatre, Manchester; Best Production at the Dublin International Theatre Festival and a Fringe First Award at the Edinburgh Fringe Festival in 2005 for his production of *Knots* for CoisCeim Dance Theatre; Herald Angel Award for Outstanding Choreographic Achievement at the Edinburgh International Festival for his work on *Strictly Dandia* for Tamasha Theatre Company.

Rob Tannion Director/Choreographer

Rob is one of the UK's most influential physical theatre practitioners. Alongside his work with Stan Won't Dance, Rob has maintained his influential profile as a director, choreographer and performer. Choreography and direction credits include: *Fragil*, *Princesas* (Karlik Danza Teatro, Spain); *Crece* (Teatro Circo Price, Madrid); *InFame* (Excentrica Produccines, Seville); *Stand and Stare* (Fairgame Theatre, UK); *Sinking Water* (APA, Lyric Theatre, Hong Kong); *Looking for*

Love (StopGAP Dance Company); *Take Action: Stunt Dancing*, *Intent* (Southbank Centre, London); *Apparition* (Klaus Obermaier); *Fetish: Stories* (City Hall Theatre, Hong Kong); and *Dinner* (National Palace of Culture, Sofia).

In 2005/6 he was Associate Choreographer for the original stage version of *Lord of the Rings*, which premiered in Toronto in March 2006 and won a 2006 Dora Maver Moore Award for Choreography. He collaborated with Peter Darling in the casting process for *Billy Elliot* the Musical in 2003/4. As a performer, collaborations have included projects with Austrian cross-media artist Klaus Obermaier, *Enter Achilles*, *Bound to Please*, *The Happiest Day of My Life*, *The Cost of Living* (DV8 Physical Theatre), *Noise of Time*, *Strange Poetry* (Complicité) and *Critical Mass* (Russell Maliphant Company).

Patrick Neate Writer

Patrick Neate is a novelist, scriptwriter, critic and poet. His first novel, *Musungu Jim and the Great Chief Tuloko* (Penguin, 2000) won a Betty Trask Award, while *Twelve Bar Blues* (Penguin, 2001) won the Whitbread Novel Prize. His latest, *Jerusalem* (Penguin, 2009), has been described by *The Sunday Telegraph* as, 'A corrosive and blistering satire on colonialism and an eloquent, angry and relevant novel that speaks its own truth to power.'

Patrick's nonfiction includes *Where You're At: Notes from the Frontline of a Hip-Hop Planet* (Bloomsbury, 2003), which won the National Book Critics Circle Award for Criticism in the USA, and *Culture Is Our Weapon* (LAB, 2006 with Damian Platt), an analysis of the transformative possibilities of music among the drug gangs of Rio de Janeiro.

When not being eloquent or angry, Patrick tries to remain relevant as the founder of Book Slam, London's best-known (and best) night of words and music, that has featured artists from Adele to Zadie Smith. Originally commissioned by Channel 4, *BABEL* explores the limitations of contemporary language and the ways in which, for all the perceived liberties of British society, our freedom of speech is compromised.

COMPANY BIOGRAPHIES

Andy Purves Lighting Design

Andy holds an MA in lighting design and theatre making from Central School of Speech and Drama where he also tutors in lighting. He is a lighting designer and creative technician working primarily in visual and movement-based theatre, circus and on projects in found space. Recent projects include *Stockholm*, *Othello*, *Pool (No Water)* and *Dirty Wonderland* (Frantic Assembly); *Moby Dick*, *Cooped*, *Stiff* and *Bless* (Spymonkey); lighting designs for Circus Space/ London Youth Circus; *The Erpingham Camp* (Brighton Festival); *Ida Barr* and *Office Party* (Barbican Pit, London); *Frankenstein* (The Royal Theatre, Northampton); lighting for *La Clique* at The Hippodrome and The Roundhouse, London; *The Wolves in the Walls* and *Home Inverness* (National Theatre of Scotland); *Outré* and *Ren-Sa* (Array).

Gareth Fry Sound Design

Gareth trained at the Central School of Speech and Drama in theatre design. His recent work includes: *Pains of Youth*, *The Cat in the Hat* (NT); *Endgame* (Complicité); *The Fahrenheit Twins* (Told By An Idiot); *After Dido* (ENO); *Dancing at Lughnasa* (Old Vic). Other work includes: *Waves* (Olivier Award 2007); *Some Trace of Her*, *Fram*, *Women of Troy*, *A Matter of Life and Death* (Kneehigh); *Attempts on her Life*, *The Overwhelming* (New York); *Theatre of Blood* (Improbable); *Fix Up*, *Iphigenia at Aulis*, *Three Sisters*, *Ivanov* and *The Oresteia* (National Theatre); *Black Watch* (National Theatre of Scotland [Olivier Award 2009]); *Shun-kin*, *Noise of Time* (Emerson String Quartet); *Strange Poetry* (LA Philharmonic Orchestra); *Mnemonic* (Complicité); *The Swing Left*, *Tangle*, *Zero Degrees* and *Drifting* (Unlimited Theatre); *Astronaut* (Theatre O); *The Cost of Living* (DV8 at Tate Modern); *The Flowerbed*, *The Bull and Giselle* (Fabulous Beast Dance Theatre); *O Go My Man*, *Talking to Terrorists* and *Macbeth* (Out of Joint); *The City*, *Harvest*, *Forty Winks*, *Under the Whaleback*, *Night Songs*, *Face to the Wall*, *Redundant*, *Mountain Language*, *Ashes to Ashes* and *The Country* (Royal Court); *How Much is Your Iron?* and *The Jewish Wife* (Young Vic Brecht Fest); *Shadowmouth* and *The Romans in Britain* (Sheffield Crucible). Radio includes: *The Overwhelming* (BBC Radio 3); *OK Computer* and *Jump* (BBC Radio 4). He also designs the music and sound systems for Somerset House's ice rink.

Matt Spencer Video Design

Matt graduated in dance (Bretton Hall 1999), worked as a choreographer for three years, joined the David Glass Ensemble and started touring as a sound and AV technician. A few years and several continents later, Matt found his groove producing video projection designs, animations and films for dance and theatre companies. Matt produced video designs for the Stan Won't Dance productions *Sinner* and *Revelations* and has worked with Liam away from the company on *Absolute Beginners* (Lyric Hammersmith), *Great*

Expectations (Library Theatre), *The Magic Flute* (English Touring Opera), and with Rob on *Take Action: Stunt Dancing* (Royal Festival Hall), *Crece '08 & '09* (Teatro Circo Price), and *Fragil* (Karlik Danza Teatro). Additional credits include: *Rock n' Roll, The Good Soul of Szechuan* (Library Theatre); *Feeble Minds* (Spare Tyre); *The Doubtful Guest* (Hoipolloi); *Can Any Mother Help Me?* (Foursight Theatre); *Moon Behind The Clouds* (Lunasea); *Disembodied, The Chimp that Spoke* (David Glass Ensemble); *A Fine Balance, Child of the Divide, The Trouble with Asian Men, Lyrical MC*, and *Sweet Cider* (Tamasha); *Slamdunk, Mass Carib, An African Cargo* (Nitro); *The Arab & the Jew* (Gecko); Transitions Dance Co. (Laban); *Dido Queen of Carthage* (Angels in the Architecture); *Inchoate, The Real Lavender Hill Mob* (Fleur Darkin); *BHP* (Online Television); *Together Higher* (Ensemble Films, Vietnam); *Prey taa toke* (World Vision, Cambodia). Matt is also Associate Director of Kieran Sheehan Dance Theatre, responsible for developing film and animation for live performance.

Nathaniel Parchment
Performer

Nathaniel received his dance training at Lewisham College before joining the National Youth Dance Company, where he performed works by Mark Baldwin, Henry Oguike and Jonathan Lunn. He then went on to complete the B.A. Hons programme at London Contemporary Dance School. Since graduating Nathaniel has worked as a performer, choreographer and director, for theatre, film and site-specific works. Nathaniel has worked for Rashpal Singh Bansal for the 2005 Robin Howard Commission at The Place, Vena Ramphal as part of the *Firsts* programme at the Royal Opera House, with Gauri Sharma Tripati for Akademi South Asian Dance UK, with Shobana Jeyasingh Dance Company for Dance Umbrella and with DV8 Physical Theatre. Recent work has included fashion photography and film projects in collaboration with dance photographer and lighting designer Mathew Hale and menswear designer Asger Juel Larsen.

Moreno Solinas Performer

Moreno trained at the London Contemporary Dance School. He became an apprentice with Bonachela Dance Company, and joined DV8 Physical Theatre for the restaging of their production *To Be Straight With You*. He is a co-founder of SU dance project, which presents dance installations internationally, and of HIRU, which promotes contemporary dance and cultural exchanges between Sardinia, London and the Basque Country. In 2010 Moreno will create a new choreographic work funded by Jardin d'Europe and the Hungarian government.

Hugh Stanier Performer

Hugh joined 2Faced Dance Company in 2003. He gained early performance experience with them at the Edinburgh Fringe Festival and went on to train at Northern School of Contemporary Dance. Since graduating he has toured with 2Faced Dance Company, JOON Dance Company, and recently with

Tempered Body. Hugh has recently trained in free running and 'Tricking'.

Dan Watson Performer

Dan began his career dancing with StopGAP Dance Company, working with them for seven years, performing the works of Hofesh Shechter, Rob Tannion and Nathalie Pernette amongst others. During that time he also danced for Retina Dance, Protein Dance, Green Candle, Seven Sisters Group and the international improvisation collective 5 Men Dancing, with whom he still performs. More recently he has worked with Evolving Motion (Formally Cathy Seago and dancers) and Slung Low (The Lowry, Salford and Barbican, London) and continues to work with Leeds-based Motion Manual. His first solo work *Semi Detached* premiered at Brighton Fringe Festival 2009.

Matthew Winston
Performer

Matthew began his training at Laban, completing his degree with first class honours. During that time he was a member of the National Youth Dance Company, performing work by Wayne McGregor and Sheron Wray. He then spent a year at London Contemporary Dance School as a member of EDge, the postgraduate dance company, performing work by Trisha Brown, Ben Wright and Kerry Nicholls. Since graduating, Matthew has worked with Bare Bones Dance Company, Matthew Bourne's New Adventures, and is a founding member of Ben Wright's company, Bgroup. He has also worked in opera, taught classes and workshops, and completed his MA at London Contemporary Dance School. Most recently, Matthew has been working with theatre director Richard Jones on a production of *Rumpelstiltskin* for six dancers.

Ellie Beedham Executive Director

Ellie is a founder member of Stan Won't Dance. Her projects for the company include four UK and US/ Canadian tours of *Sinner* (which was nominated for a Tapa Dora Award), the UK production and tour of *Revelations*, and two site-specific works, *Skylon Spirits* and *Off The Wall* for the reopening of the Royal Festival Hall, London, in summer 2007. Ellie is the Producer at The Place and previously worked as Head of Communications at Laban, Head of Marketing and Sales at the Lyric Hammersmith and with DV8 Physical Theatre on the Sydney Olympics Arts Festivals commission, *The Cost of Living*.

Jon Woodley Production Manager

Jon trained at RADA and has worked for many theatres and companies, including Regent's Park Open Air Theatre, Northcott Theatre Exeter, Bill Kenwright Ltd, The Abbey Theatre (National Theatre of Ireland), Cameron Mackintosh, RSC, Royal Opera House, and Universal Shows Dubai. Recent productions include: *A Dolls House* (Exeter); *Hello Dolly!*, *The Importance of Being Earnest*, *The Tempest*, *Much Ado About Nothing* (Regent's Park); *Peter Pan*, Agatha Christie's *Spiders Web*, *The Vortex* (Apollo Theatre); *Absurd Person Singular* (Garrick Theatre); *The Concert They Never*

Gave, Sleuth, *And Then There Were None*, *Half A Sixpence*, *Kicking a Dead Horse* (Dublin & Almeida); and *Terminus*.

Andy Guard Technical Stage Manager

Andy trained at Central Saint Martins College of Art and Design and previously worked in the Fashion & Textiles industry before moving into Stage Management. He has stage managed for Regents Park Open Air Theatre, Bill Kenwright Ltd, Northcott Theatre Exeter, Theatre Royal Windsor and Shunt Theatre Company. Recent productions include *Much Ado About Nothing*, *The Tempest*, *The Importance of Being Earnest*, *Hello Dolly!*, *Murder On Air*, *An Ideal Husband*, *A Doll's House*, *Tropicana*, and *Amato Saltone*.

Chris Reid Sound Technician

Chris studied Creative Sound Production at the University of Abertay, Dundee. He has worked in Scottish Theatre for most of his career to date, before moving to London early in 2009. Recent productions include *A Streetcar Named Desire*, *The Snow Queen*, *Tam O' Shanter*, *The Mystery Of Irma Vep*, *Pinocchio* (Perth Theatre), *Much Ado About Nothing*, *The Tempest*, *The Importance of Being Earnest*, *Hello Dolly!* (Regents Park Open Air Theatre), *The House Of Bernarda Alba* (The National Theatre of Scotland).

Tiffany Evans Marketing

Tiffany has been working in arts marketing for 20 years. She is a freelance marketing consultant working predominantly with contemporary dance and dance theatre companies. Along with Stan Won't Dance, current clients include Dance Touring Partnership, Vincent Dance Theatre and Shobana Jeyasingh Dance Company. She has worked with DV8 Physical Theatre, Ultima Vez, Australian Dance Theatre, Jasmin Vardimon, Fabulous Beast and Hofesh Shechter. Other clients have included Sadler's Wells, Dance Umbrella, Rambert Dance Company and Siobhan Davies Dance Company. Before going freelance in 1998 she worked full time for V-TOL Dance Company, Wycombe Swan, English Touring Opera, Bath International Festival and the Natural Theatre Company.

Hanna Streeter Administration & Education

Hanna recently joined Stan Won't Dance whilst completing her Masters in Arts Policy and Management at Birkbeck, University of London. During this time she also worked as a Youth and Community Intern at Arcola Theatre, helping to run the Hackney Youth Theatre Festival and an inter-generational project with ATC. She also worked with Ellie Beedham on the 2009 Greenwich and Docklands International Festival. Having previously gained a first class B.A. Hons degree in Performing Arts from the University of Chichester, Hanna also has experience in devising and performing her own theatre work.

Introduction

I sit and write this Introduction on the eve of going into rehearsal. The moment just before a new project begins always spawns a strange mix of emotions – trepidation, excitement, eagerness, fear, and an overriding feeling of pure blind panic! Never in my career have these feelings been more profound than as they are going into rehearsals for BABEL. The reason? The piece of text you are holding in your hand right now.

What is it? An epic poem? A theatrical script? A rant? A rap? Or just the ramblings of a hip-hop hyperactive madman?

At this stage, I don't know. And to be honest, I don't really care. Because what I DO know is that it is the work of a skilled literary swordsman and my acute cocktail of emotions stem primarily from a great desire to do justice to this incredible, controversial and passionate collection of words.

I first came across Patrick Neate's work in a Travelodge hotel room in Manchester in 2005. Rob Tannion and myself were on tour performing *Sinner*, and as usual found ourselves, post show, ensconced in our respective hotel rooms channel-flicking. Suddenly, out of the late night drivel thinly disguised as entertainment, emerged a remarkable voice of sanity. I was confronted by a London shaven-headed 'geezer' spouting verse at me through the TV screen that made me (for the first time in a long time) sit up and pay attention. That man was Patrick Neate and the words were the birth of *BABEL*.

The program was part of Channel 4's *Made in Britain* series and focused on the idea that, for all the perceived liberties of British society, a mix of materialism, the single agenda media and restrictive ideas of political correctness have compromised true freedom of speech.

Halfway through, the ad-break came. My phone rang and a tired but excited voice on the other end asked me if I was watching the program. Rob was transfixed in the same way as myself.

Jump a couple of years and we were pulling together ideas for a new Stan Won't Dance piece. I was in the Tate Modern leafing through photography books for creative inspiration when I came across a photograph of what appeared to be a young man falling and apparently about to hit the ground at high speed. It was taken by a French photographer called Denis Darzacq, and further investigation revealed that this photograph was just one of a whole series he had taken of young hip-hop street dancers mid flight. The images represented an entire generation in freefall, ignored by society, their energy untapped and unused. Though taken in Paris, the banal modern architecture gave a sense that the images could have been taken anywhere in Europe. In every picture the streets were completely empty and behind the leaden expressionless falling bodies, all doors and window shutters were firmly closed. Would anyone even notice them hit the ground? Would anyone care?

Of course Darzacq's work is open to multiple interpretations, but for me it hit home that in today's society we are allowing our youth to become ignored, feared and left to crash to their downfall.

As I left the gallery, I was immediately confronted by the headline of another young man being stabbed to death on the streets of London. I jumped on a bus and listened to a group of teenage girls 'babbling' in an indecipherable language that seemed to be composed of nothing more than phrases such as 'Innit?' 'You know what I mean?' 'No way!' and 'Bad!' And in a sudden convergence of artistic and social alignments, Patrick's words exploded in my head once again.

What followed were months of trying to track Patrick down, a series of e-mails trying to persuade him that we weren't crazy stalkers, and then a final face-to-face meeting to bully him into accepting our proposal of writing a full length piece for the company. He accepted. And now, a year later, I sit in my panic-stricken state of being, trying to write an introduction to the fruits of that labour.

By the time you read this, Patrick's words will have been raped and molested in the dishevelled bed we call the rehearsal process, and, all being well, a few weeks later, a conjoined twin of text and choreography will have been born of the union.

Theatre for me is about raising questions. If we have any intention in the physicalisation of Patrick's words, it is not to attempt to provide any answers to the many questions that he raises, but simply to generate further questioning. If we can achieve that, then I will feel we will have done justice to his razor-sharp sword.

Listen. See. Notice. Question.

Liam Steel

Babel is a collaboration between Patrick Neate and Stan Won't Dance; the text as it is published here is not as it is used in the production. Patrick's text provided a blueprint and starting point for devising and was subsequently re-structured and edited into a piece of dance-theatre where the spoken and choreographic language are completely integral to each other. There are intentionally no staging directives: the stage design and performance should be devised according to the vision of the director and creative team.

Patrick Neate
BABEL

OBERON BOOKS
LONDON

First published in 2010 by Oberon Books Ltd
521 Caledonian Road, London N7 9RH
Tel: 020 7607 3637 / Fax: 020 7607 3629
e-mail: info@oberonbooks.com
www.oberonbooks.com

A catalogue record for this book is available from the British Library.

ISBN: 978-1-8400298-1-9

Cover photography by Brian Benson

Printed in Great Britain by CPI Antony Rowe, Chippenham

babel. *noun.* a confused noise made by a number of voices.

We are living in Babel. Did you know that?

I ask you this –
In our British cosmopolis
The progeny of homogeny
Do we notice?
Or do we just see ourselves reflected
In the shimmering windows of this monument to …
To what?
To freedom of choice?
Is that the freedom to speak in only one voice?
Because now
Babel's built
And still we don't notice
As we're blinded by the vanity
The profanity
Of the false idols
That we worship idly –

We speak one language
The consequence of a conspiracy
Of idiocy
Between the establishment – so-called – who decided it
And the rest of us who may have denied, decried or
derided it
But were ultimately rendered apathetic
And acquiescent
By our position outside
Of it

And in this final confirmation
Of globalisation
We don't just say what we think
We think what we say –
And we're all saying the same thing

We hardly use words any more,
Just soundbites

Adverts, brands
The label is our Babel
And the fable's been made true
So I say –
'Please God! Come down to earth
And whisper forgotten tongues in our ear
That we might hear forgotten lessons
To lessen the shock of the earthquake
Which *will* happen
And flatten
Our beautiful, awesome, pointless tower.'

There remains a certain power
And elegance in all this mediocrity …

Do we notice that entombed in Babel's foundations
Are the corpses of a thousand arguments undebated
Whether related or unrelated,
Often conflated,
Frequently mutilated and aborted,
Or contorted and resorted to only by those of the species
We've classified
'Genus extremist'?
– Now that's a condition which when detected
Has to be immediately
Politically corrected.

The greatest trick the devil ever played?
It was persuading us not to talk about him for fear of
offending one another …

We live in a nation
Where liberality equates with banality
Where the political correctness directive
Too often
Leaves us all ineffective
Where morality is reduced to soundbites
Of such vacuous generality

That we can't examine them
For fear of embarrassment
Where discussions of what we believe
Are necessarily outré
And leave intelligent company distraught
Because they require us to define ourselves
And so we find ourselves
Caught short
Suddenly aware of what we're missing –
That is, a pot to piss in

Are we not racist
Sexist
Homophobic
Fundamentalist
Terrorists
Because our language has the consideration
Of a liberal education?

We saw the bullet, but no-one bit it
So, will anyone stand shoulder to shoulder with us
And admit it?
Our isms?
They're the faces of a prism
Shooting opinions
At all degrees
Of all colours and creeds
And sexualities.
And we could agree
To disagree
And just
Trust
In the difference
That makes us, us –
Please
Can't it be like that?

If we don't see eye to eye

Isn't that fine
So long as we close our mouths
Open our minds
Kick back
And relax
Into facts (so-called)
That deny other so-called facts?
We can design and refine our tactics
Until we have an hypothesis
Which we're prepared to contend
Then – guess what? –
We're in a debate.
Remember them?

What if our words don't encapsulate
Our ideas
But create them?
What if our fears, for example, are not fears at all
But bubbles of saliva popping on
The tongue
Upon which we hung
Our hopes?

Can we cope if the reality of modern love
Doesn't carry the thread of that emotion above which we
once held only the divine
And, instead, expresses a simple lack of vocabulary
Leaving us scrabbling to define
The night we met
And drank too much wine
And struggled to reproduce
Through barriers chemical
And rubber?

Or
To put it another way
What if when we say
'I love you'

It's for no better reason
Than that's what Ross said to Rachel
And Rachel to Ross
In a half-remembered episode of Friends
And any real meaning that we might intend is lost?
What if we tear away
The layers of irony
In which our heart is mummified
And don't find something that beats with life
And pulses with that bloody thrill that cannot be sated,
But something shriveled and still and sadly desiccated?

What if?

What if the sacrifice of collectivity
And associated responsibilities
On the altar of individuality
With the cool knife of consumption
Has altered us in ways unforeseen?
What if the assumption of self-identification
Has been
An obfuscation
And through the horrifying processes
Of personal acquisition
i.e. free market capitalism
We find ourselves –
Accidentally –
In the position
Of the single-celled organism
Back in the primeval pond
Capable of no greater sophistication
Than to feel a stimulus and respond?
And love – tender love! – as it was once conceived
Is gone.
Emily Dickinson wrote:
'That love is all there is
Is all we know of love
It is enough –'

That might have been true
When we knew what love meant
And hadn't learned to mangle our meaning
For the sake
Of our tangled tongues
And hung ourselves out to dry
On the hook of the definitive modern vice –
Which is what?
Our singular refusal to sacrifice
And there's suddenly not a single 'if' in sight …

We live in a nation where 3 million citizens
Are members of adultfriendfinder.com –
Think about it –
That's quite something to discover
That one in ten is looking for an illicit, online lover
And maybe we're just dogs on heat
Who find nothing more exciting
Than joyless sex with a stranger in Brighton
And our idea of a good time
Is dogging in a lay-by
Outside Ashton-Under-Lyme
But isn't it much more likely
That 3 million lost souls are looking for a human touch
And, starved of intimacy,
Apply themselves with alacrity
To the task
Of finding its shadow and pray
That this, at least, is not too much
To ask?

Social networking sites
Sexual or otherwise
Are they really the lights
At the end of the tunnel
Of social dislocation?
Or are they symptoms
Possibly even causes

Of increasing isolation
As we Twitter our emotions
And update our mood on Facebook?
And look
How we never refuse a friend request on MySpace
But ignore our upstairs or downstairs neighbour
For fear they might invade our space?
Who knew that you, frail as you are, wanted nothing more
Than to be viewed on YouTube
To have your shit read on your blog
That you dumped in the great
Virtual
Bog?
'This is the journal of a single woman in Macclesfield
who's fed up of being ignored? Warning! Read no further if
you're easily bored!'
Is this really the height of our expression
Or simply further example of a terrible new repression?

In our society
Information is endless
And, therefore, relative.
Give me any premise
And I can find
Too much supporting material
Online
For you to read
In one lifetime.
Isn't that the epitome
Of madness?

But set that aside a moment
And consider instead
That our children spend on average
6 hours in front of a computer screen every day
Where, once, they may have read.
Consider the distinction of process
Between following a narrative

And leaping from link to link
In a way that is, at best, reliant on instinct.
While a story requires direction
And the necessity to connect cause and effect,
The experience of the internet
Is intrinsically driven by the ill-considered mores of an
individual's decision
And so, intrinsically,
Rides roughshod over the formalities of logical precision.
Are we not, therefore, living in a nation
That's raising a generation
That has no grasp of context
And is consequently, more or less,
Intrinsically vexed
A generation that understands only sensation and desire –
Indulged on one side
And, on the other,
Denied?

So it's no wonder we're left with
Children who paint themselves orange and eat themselves
sick
And starve themselves sicker and think themselves thick
And dress themselves naked, and dream themselves cupid
And drink themselves silly, and fuck themselves stupid
And kill each other with guns that they hired five pounds a
time
Or kill themselves in knots of misery online
And they're old before their time, and they're younger than
they seem
And they're quick to join a gang but they'd never join a
team
But Chlamydia United, as they swop their STDs
As they pay-as-they-go in venereal disease.
And you can never hit a kid, so watch them hit each other
Never intervene, just step back and blame the mother
Turn a deaf ear to their screams and dose them Ritalin
Diagnose a syndrome for our state they're living in

And cherish their psychosis and brief narcotic smiles
Better that than they go outside and risk the paedophiles –
And if we love our kids so much, why is it their fate
To be the secret, unredeemed objects of our hate?
No wonder our kids are having kids, and their kids now call you mum
And they've got so much to say even as they're rendered dumb
Because they know everything and nothing, but at least they've an excuse
Because the desperate, ridiculous, unedifying truth
Is that, if not what we've chosen, this is what we've allowed
All in the name of 'freedom', is this supposed to make us proud?

We live in a nation
Where you can pick a poor man from a line-up
On the grounds that he's fat
Think a minute –
What kind of topsy-turvy country
Can produce a fact like that?
Look in the poor man's fridge
Do you see an absence of food or a rude procession of the processed
And nothing that photosynthesized
Nor drew a living breath?
And step back from that fridge, perch on the settee
Do you think you won't see a Wii
A universal remote control, Sky+, HDTV?
So how will you know the geezer's poor unless his buttocks scar an armchair
Or, among the clutter on the sideboard, you find a lottery ticket somewhere?
No, just look for a book
See what the poor man's reading.
And if you can't find one?
You know where this is leading –
Because poverty in this country is rarely about hunger nor

even sufficiency
But contemporary culture's ruthless efficiency
In stripping an underclass of any aspiration
With a mixture of fatty foods
And under-education …

So the government launches 'Food For Life',
A campaign to explain to the institutionally thick
That the society they're living in is making them
institutionally sick
And the supermarkets are recruited to display fresh fruit at
the till
Because, that way, we will surely all eat our five a day –
And what's it got to do with communication?
Only this –
When judging the value of a message
Do we not consider the motivation of the messenger?
In which case
Surely the state and its bedfellows
That thrive on citizens who are fat and dumb
And, above all, numb
Can never be expected to dictate how we may become
Thin, clever and, above all,
Awake

We live in a nation where
White kids want to be black
Asian kids want to be black
And black kids are killed for being black
And Asians for being Asian
And even whites for being white

And let's not get started on the Brazilian
Who comes to London town
To be shot dead
On the Underground
For the crime of being brown

And yet any debate about race
Has been replaced
By kindness and consensus
That frequently leaves the abused defenceless –

The police are institutionally racist
We can all agree
And shake our heads disapprovingly
But what's strange is
Nothing changes
Because
Our protests have been rendered powerless
Diluted in this slurry of verbiage
Dissolved before they can be resolved
And ultimately the worry is
That arguments remain un-argued and this has got to stop
Because it's up to us to pick up the ball the politicians
dropped

We live in a nation
Where boys of all races
With sneers on their faces
Drink alcohol apparently named after Gladiators
'Ice', 'Thunder', 'Lightning'
And take drugs apparently rendered harmless
By their acronyms
'MDMA', 'GHB', 'THC'
They sit outside suburban petrol stations
And in a feat of imagination
Dream themselves MCs
And then see a girl
Crossing the street
And kiss their teeth
And dismiss her as a bitch
And that's the closest we get to scratching the itch
We call multiculturalism

We live in a nation

Where to be gay should be more or less painless
So long as you're fashionable
Or, preferably, famous
Perhaps the homosexual is
A modern minstrel
Who sparkles on primetime TV
And claims political purpose for comedy
That reinforces stereotypes so successfully
That he can fit snugly in the box of men who like cocks
And, for all that glitter,
Ultimately fails
To tell anything
But the same old fairytales

We live in a nation
Where cheap bouquets
Are stacked a dozen deep
On street corners
Memorials
To warn us
Of the last attack
By the enemy within
That pack of hood rats
Coursing masculinity
Living like they're immortal
And dying like they're not

Yesterday
They egged each other on
With feral shrieks
These freaks of culture
MTV junkies
Hip hop monkeys
Vultures on the carcass of progress
Maggots on the flesh of good taste
They chased a young man at full tilt
And buried a knife to the hilt
In his chest –

And there's no use crying over spilt life, right?

They were compelled and propelled by hate
Because he wasn't from their estate
That's the message that they send
That he was from the wrong ends
And he met the wrong end
The wrong end

And now
Look at us!
How eloquent we are in our grieving
Leaving condolences scrawled on walls
On messageboards
And MySpace and Facebook and Bebo ...
And flowers
Endless flowers left
As if for a dead princess
(Whether Diana or, now,
A sign of the progress that we've made, Jade).
We are encouraged to express ourselves
And we do
With epithets
Learned from Oprah or Jeremy Kyle
Littlejohn or even Pilger
But aren't we deceived by what we've done
When even this outpouring of grief is received wisdom?
We know
We must show
What we feel
And we can say anything, it seems,
Except – No.
I. Will. Not. Let. This. Happen.

'Knife crime is up!'
We wail
Through the pages of the Daily Mail
Has any nation ever managed more successfully the subtle

interaction
Between extreme self-loathing and supreme self-
satisfaction?

Still, it's arguably more worthwhile than complaining
About someone we've never heard of being rude to
someone we've forgotten about on a show we never listen
to.
Thank God the newspapers publish
This rubbish
Because how else would we know to be offended by words
We wouldn't otherwise have heard?

One month apart.
Two headlines.
Same newspaper.
2009.
One: 'Coffee causes cancer'
Two: 'Coffee cures cancer'
Who knew?
And who's saying this?
Of course it's that unnamed but irrefutable group,
'scientists'
And, assuming both can't be true,
We're buying that paper to see
There's no discernible carcinogenic outcome
To drinking coffee –
Are we children? Do we really need the media stick and
carrot
To learn to repeat these untruths with all the wit of an ill-
considered parrot?

What if our language itself is no longer fit for purpose?
What if our monoglot nation is lost in translation?
What if our tongue is cracked like a Chinese DVD
That you buy for 50p
From an entrepreneur/crook/immigrant/refugee?
What if there is a fault line in contemporary English

That diminishes the correlation between intention and
meaning
Until each and every word is secretly deceiving
Not just those being addressed
But also those who do their best
To express what is true?

George Orwell wrote, 'During times of universal deceit,
telling the truth becomes a revolutionary act.'
But what if the words simply don't allow it?
What if 'true', in the currency of our contemporary tongue,
No longer has value?

What if? Whatif? Wottif?

One man's terrorist is another man's freedom fighter
What do you think? Yes?
One man's politician is another man's terrorist
Good. Get it off your chest.
One man's cop is another man's player hater
One man's president is another man's dictator
One man's memory is another man's history
One man's science is another man's mystery
One man's evil is another man's evolution
One man's terror is another man's revolution
One man's fundamentalist is another man's infidel
And one man's relativist is another man's 'Well, you know,
at the end of the day, when all's said and done, it's a game
of two halves as well ...'

The test
Of our progress
As an advanced economy
Has been the abstraction of value from utility through
money
And yet there is no gold standard
For money is an article of faith
Now strafed by doubts

About its ability to support
Its claims –
And isn't language the same
Its meaning dependent upon consent
In which that which is meant is agreed to be meant?
And hasn't such a situation,
Ripe for exploitation
By those who define themselves experts in manipulation,
Been fatally undermined?
The public find themselves owning high street banks
Which, by way of thanks, refuse to lend us our own money
And, with the blessing of the treasury,
Sell off their best bits, like breast and thigh,
And leave us nibbling around the chicken head and
avoiding its beady eye.
It would almost be funny if we weren't so damn poor
And can fall back on nothing more than a decent metaphor
For this nation in a credit crunch of communication

Listerine! The Imperial Leather is coming
For Sure
It's Head And Shoulders rise above the Colgate
As its Pearl Drops, Pantene
It's Right Guard Lynx Beneath the Arm And Hammer
Insignia
And it cries out, 'Elvive!'
But the battlefield's a Body Shop – Mostly Men – so
Fructis!
And as much as we might Toilet Duck, Wash And Go
We'll never get Macleans away
From this … this what?
Badedas?
Or do I mean Adidas?
Jesus!

'Because I'm worth it'
What am I worth?
'It'

Third person. Pronoun. Neuter.
I am worth IT. Shampoo.
I should hope so too.

Nike,
Can you Fila memory of a New Balance in this Timberland
As the Converse Hilfiger with the Carhartt Fruit of the
Looms over the FCUK
And we wonder DKNY?

Lycos we've gone Microsoft
Can't you Intel?
Stuck in our Microsoft Office
At our Microsoft Works
And our only Outlook Express is from our Windows 7
Yahoo! We broadband of brothers! We podcast of
thousands! We Internet Explorers on Safari who are iPhone
app to wikithis and wikithat and Twitter the hope that
information might save us …
But there is no Netscape now they've got us by the
Googles!

IMap RSS, Binhex, POP DNS, Slip SMTP and Gif spam
You don't like what we do?
WTF? OMG! ROTFLMAO and FAQ too …

We see a Lidl Mace through Waitrose of Somerfields
Tesco!
But Mum's gone to Iceland
And we have no Sunny Delight, no Fruit 'n' Fibre, no Gold
Blend left
We're just Slimfast
Diet Coke
Lean Cuisine
St Ivel Shape
I can't believe it's not butter.
But Asda our Anchor? our Country Life?
It's to be a Lurpak of Pop Tarts

You see?

They say you can't fool all the people all the time
But what if the deception itself
Has gagged the rest and left them
Speechless?

We champion freedom and democracy
But we don't know what they are
We suspect they're something about Mickey D's
Opening in Kandahar
And the freedom and democracy? This is what really
tickles
It's my democratic right to say 'Big Mac, hold the pickles.'
Because they're just buzz words that make us buzz
As other words make us hiss
Democracy – Buzz!
Dictator – Hiss!
And it goes on like this

In fact the words are barely words at all
But really further branding
And see if you can follow us
Because it's our understanding
That as Babel is constructed
So it's lead to the condition
Where we no longer seek the truth
Just brand recognition

Freedom is about choice
Democracy about representation
So we're free to choose to represent ourselves on blogs
Or forums
Even demonstrations
But we live in a nation where freedom of speech
Now means the freedom to be ignored
As our leaders look the other way and wait until we're
bored

Or distracted by the story
Of another fallen star
Socially contracted to celebrity as we are
Culture? Shared experience?
It now has no greater depth than Z pop star slept with Y
model who was previously dating X

Churchill claimed that democracy was the best of a bad
bunch
He also said he'd be sober in the morning –
Promises, promises …

Blair became Middle East Peace Envoy
And, in one instant,
Destroyed not just meaningful politics
But comedy

We launched a war that was 'legal but not legitimate'
That's not semantics but reverse punning
In which two words sound different but mean precisely the
same …

And of course it would be funny if it was all a game
But now we're looking the other way from those acting in
our name
And of course war is a game in the way its advertised
And they are, of course, 'our boys' so they can't be
criticized
'Start thinking soldier', they say and so you do
But does it look like an advert for the Army or 'Call Of
Duty Two: Modern Warfare'?
And our boys all own Playstations and they've little grasp
of context
And our boys love our nation and haven't many other
prospects
And our boys are sent to fight to settle unknown scores
And we must be proud of our boys despite our shame
about each war

And its not like on the X Box
Where your ammunition's endless
And our boys are ill-equipped
And our boys are left defenceless
And our boys come home in body bags
And thousands gather in respect on the streets of Wootton
Bassett
As we struggle to connect the cynicism of government
Who silence dissenting noise
By implying it equates
With criticism of our boys
But we know the men who chose the playing field
The same men who chose the toys
The same men who've now forgotten
That our boys are simply boys
And the deception is now so complete
Even the deceivers are deceived
By the lies that seem encoded
Within our linguistic genes

And its not just our language that slips into babble
Scrabble through our visual vocabulary
And find numerous symbols that hold no fixed position
And thus signify both one thing and its binary opposition
Like –
I was walking the streets of London's fashionable London
the other day
And I was surprised to see Z pop star
Loitering in a doorway
More surprised still when she greeted me like an old friend
And, being British, and eager not to offend
I greeted her likewise
She was wearing her pop star outfit –
Hotpants, a bustier, and boots to her thighs
A silver cross nestled in her cleavage
And her hair pulled back in a Croydon facelift that
narrowed her eyes.
We talked for a while

And she seemed to enjoy my company, revelling in the compliments I paid
And laughing at jokes I hadn't realized I'd made.
Comprehension, therefore, came slowly
Only dawning, at last, when she asked for fifty quid
To blow me.
The truth was this wasn't a pop star
But a prostitute
And, cute though she was, I felt like I'd been played.
Indeed, I was dismayed to discover
That the oldest profession and the most taboo (i.e. a professional lover)
Should now be indistinguishable from what is, in our society
The height of virtue (i.e. a celebrity)
So I sidestepped her affections
Stood back
And, spotting a copper coming in the other direction,
Complained that I was distressed by the way she was dressed.
Why should I have to be distracted by so much bare flesh?
It's out of place, I said
Unless displayed by an R&B chick on MTV Base.
So the policeman looked at her
And he took in her hot pants
Bustier and boots
And sniffed
As if to say, 'There's nothing I can do'
Until his eyes settled on her breasts
And finally lit up
And he tutted to himself and told her that while he could accept all the rest
She must remove the crucifix from her chest
Lest her apparent religious conviction,
Inappropriate in a secular society,
Proved a source of multicultural friction.
Of course, the poor whore was embarrassed
And I was embarrassed on her behalf

As she not only removed the cross, but put on a long coat
And covered her head with a scarf
But the PC wasn't having it
'Excuse me, miss,' he said. 'Are you a Muslim?'
And, being British and middle-class, what could I do but
laugh?
Before beating a retreat around the corner to view another
piece of monetized arse.
But I was nonetheless disturbed by what I perceived as
going on
Because when we can't tell whether an angel's fallen aren't
we living in Babylon?

It must be our symbolic language itself that confuses us
Its appropriation by the mechanisms of commercialization
Refusing us the ability
The linguistic agility
To express an idea
More meaningful
Than 'I am here. Look at me'

It's a tragedy!
– When he's thrown out of X Factor
It's the end of the world!
– When she's tossed from the Big Brother House
My life is over!
– We scream as our ambition to impale ourselves on the
 phallus of celebrity leaves us raw and saddle-sore

All our emotions are more or less ersatz
That's the price we pay
For saying what we feel even though we don't feel what we
say

But the kids outside the garage still say
Do you know what I mean?
And the fundamentalist terrorists, they say
Do you know what I mean?

And the Queen and the queens say
Do you know what I mean?
And even the politicians say
Do you know what I mean?

Ironically
This has become the epitome of oratory for the 21st
Century
In which no-one knows what anyone means
Because we're so out of touch
But everybody knows enough to know that nobody means
much
So the question becomes rhetorical
Arguably even metaphorical for our present state
At least the state of present debate
At most our nation state

It's not important what you say
But to say it long and loud
W.M.D.s
Words of Mass Distraction –
Don't they make us proud?

Yet this state is our oasis
And, therefore, QED
All that's left for us to say is
'Do you know what I mean?'
Or
'Yes we can'
Is that an answer to the question
Or affirmative – inclusive – positive
Meaningless suggestion?

Can we change?
Yes we can
Can we heal this nation?
Yes we can
Can we seize our future?

Yes we can
Can we simultaneously hold beliefs in social justice and the
free market?
In global warming and the driving season?
In low taxes and universal healthcare?
In fundamentals and religious freedom?
Can we?
Do you know what I mean?

Our tower's built ever upwards
On foundations of hot air
So keep your eyes towards the skies
You shan't look down, you wouldn't dare
We'll climb until we're Gods ourselves
And receive what we believe we're due
So, lord, let us forgive us
Who know all too well just what we do.

Here in Babel
Our great seats of learning now
Churn out drones
With aspirations toward the media
Who don't care about the world they live in
So much as their entry on Wikipedia

And even creativity is now commercially specific
With a novel, piece of art, or song
No more than a list of brands
Two hundred pages, one installation
Or two minutes long
And critics – whom I picket –
Claim it's clever, relevant, postmodern
In the way it draws attention to convention by the very
invention of its absence –
Suckers!

And in a country house hotel
Just outside the M25

Alive with the potential of a day
Away from the daily grind
We find two dozen middle-aged, white executives
From a mid-range alcohol brand
Accepting photocopied handouts from an underground,
black rapper
Whose crapulous task
Is to ask his audience to step up to the mic one by one
And, fuelled by as much of their product as they like,
RAP!
Of course, the experience is agonizing for all involved
But gradually they dissolve
Into Bacardi Breezers
Two Dogs
And Moscow Mules
The tools of their trade
That allow them to decide the precise nature
Of their WKD side.
And eventually they scatter cat-in-the-hat rhyming couplets
That amuse the booze-fuelled
And make the rapper so vexed that he almost forgets
To collect his pay cheque,
Before the middle-aged and white
Who are now so drunk and wrong
That they think they're not just sober and right
But young and black as well
Get down, throw up, make out, cop off and eventually
sleep in
And wake up hung over, but in clover
Marketing pigs in marketing shit
Who now understand it
Who've now had the 'urban' education
To sell alcopops to black girls
And, therefore, the entire adolescent population

… And the rapper gets home at some ungodly hour
raises his right fist to the mirror
And murmurs, 'Fight the power.'

Language is a code
A coherent series of symbols that grants us the tools
To best express
At home, in public, at work and in our schools
And yet this glorious capacity has fallen to the voracity of apathy
As we multinationalize, globalize, rationalize our small world
To a series of in jokes that can never be funny when everybody gets them

Or, to put it another way:
'Here comes the science' –

Our language has a unique formula with several extracts and complexes
From a mysterious (but nonetheless highly scientific) source,
Which will strengthen Babel and give our certainties new force
With up to 100 per cent more manageability
Up to 100 per cent more gloss
Up to 100 per cent more shine
Up to 100 per cent more meaning lost
And up to 100 per cent more bullshit
And why?
Because we're worth it
– Or so we assert

And our fourth estate – so-called
Our great protector
The supposed bullshit detector
Is – let me check the language of our nation's petrol stations –
A bitch.
Our press is, at best, stitched up by the establishment (so-called),

At worst seduced by self-importance that reduces it to
Portentousness
Until argument is semantic, a pedantic representation
Of what we, frankly, fat and comfortable
And pinkly in the pink, are expected to think

And in so far as we are capable of ascertaining the truth of
information
We find we've undergone a sophisticated form of
inoculation
The fact that we're allowed to speak makes us think it
matters what we say
While our basic love of luxury makes us look the other way
And the drip feed from the media has bolstered our
immunity
To allow the powers that be, and always were, to continue
with impunity
To detain without charge, and ignore international law
Denying those detained to know what they've been
detained for
And we can't support torture, so support extraordinary
rendition
Our deceptive language granting us all a deluded new
condition
Because it's not just the war on terror, every war's now
fought within
And the biggest battle is whether we accept what's
happening
As the media sate our appetites and our leaders dull our
synapses
And our comprehension of right and wrong fatally
collapses
Because we're scrabbling to get more branded stuff, in the
dirt and on the floor
And anyone can do what they want to us when we're
buckled on all fours
Of course, whatever turn history takes, history's going to
turn

But I can't bear that we'll still be fiddling when Rome
begins to burn
We know that information's everything, information is the
key
But what we need to know about information is it's quality
not quantity
And quality describes the message not the medium of
transmission
For style over content is not an acceptable position
But acceptance of exactly this is how we're now defined
It's not just the world that shrunk, but so too the collective
mind

And the leaders, standfirsts, headlines
Are all saying the same thing
And the *Guardian, Telegraph, Times*
Are all saying the same thing
And ITN, BBC, Sky
Are all saying the same thing
And even those on opposite sides
Are all saying the same thing!

They all sing from the same hymn sheet
If the words differ, the tunes match
So wherever we get our news, here's the disturbing catch –
Free thinking? We've completely forgotten what it means
Is it the name of a new Ikea range, aftershave or magazine?
It's no longer an aspiration but simply a label
So any hope of achieving it has long been taken off the
table

And I don't care that the UK is racist, sexist and
homophobic
I don't care that we think we're right and are therefore
jingoistic
In fact, while we're at it, let's be realistic
I don't care that it's classist, selfish and ever more
materialistic

I'm not even surprised by the neocolonial aspirations
We're children of history, empire – this is the British nation
So it's our heritage and it was ever thus
But I do object to our failure to address and to discuss and,
most of all, to notice that debate is overdue
Because in a nation of debators, this is something as
dangerous as it is new

Some of my best friends are black.
Some of my best friends are Muslim.
Some of my best friends are gay.
And I suspect that some of my best friends are sexist, racist,
homophobic fundamentalists as well

So I'm invited to a friend's house for supper
And, knowing me,
Unfortunately,
It will be a party of chatter-ati
Artfully disguised in all the best costumes of the well-
travelled and worldly-wise
Globalised and smug
We'll be warming our toes on Indian rugs
Resting our heads on Afghan throws that cover the backs of
armchairs
Made from Zanzibari railway tracks.
Even the drugs we take have been imported at vast expense
from four of the seven continents.
And now we are as verbally incontinent as we are insular
Somehow marooned on this peninsula of the middle-brow
middle classes of middle England
And yet, nonetheless, still we think we know best;
For this whole world is our dominion and our opinions
range from African famine
To George Bush,
From the credit crunch to climate change …

And damn, do we think we're different in our diffident
indifference,

As our language allows us to plough new fields that
shamefully yield just the same old same old
And our only agreement
– and you can bet we discuss it –
Is that charity muggers, telephone pluggers and the
squeegie men
Are not to be trusted
And Nigerian cabbies, Kosovan navvies, and the bloke
who installs our faux marble work surface
Are all on the make
And in this artery choking
Crafty smoking
Weed toking
Line of coke-ing
Good bloking
Festival of self-satisfaction
The extension of our good intentions finds the perfect
tension for abstention from the unmentionable –
That is, meaningful action.

Whatever –
This, though depressing,
Is not the point that I meant to be stressing

So: –
Having filled our faces with foodstuffs variously seared,
wilted and braised
And enjoyed a wine list courtesy of Tesco's Finest
At the end of the meal our host will produce a box of
something sweet
And someone is sure to pipe up and say:
'The honeycomb middle that weighs so little'
Or
'It's not Terry's it's mine'
Or
'Ambassador! You're really spoiling us!'
Or
'This is not just food …'

And it's at this point that I finally realize that our identity is
not defined by relationship
To the means of production or consumption
But to the means of selling: the way it is advertised.
And, despite my resolve that this hilarious comedy
Is nothing a loaded gun wouldn't solve,
I still laugh politely, nightly
When rightly I should stand up and say
'You cosy suckers!
Seduced by the perceptions and deceptions of finery
Reduced to the culturally constructed frailties of irony
Tell a proper gag!'

But I don't
Because they would gag on their food
Which wouldn't be good
And I'd never be invited back
I'd get the sack from such society that defends it propriety
with piety
Oh God, please!
Can we learn to hate the golden arches
Will we ever be sick of that swooshing Nike tick?
Because there's one simple fact we have to accommodate
Which is there's nothing abstract
In the politics of power masquerading as culture
That dominates the very way we communicate

You want evidence?
Sure. Just watch the planet shrink
As we eat the same fast food and drink the same sweet
drinks
But as we consume the same products
Suckling the same sow
See how we communicate worse than ever
And that pig will surely roll over to squash a piglet or two
And we never even notice

So
What do we do?
Is the only solution revolution?
Do we storm the newspapers
Television stations
And other media?
Do we close down Twitter, Facebook and Wikipedia
Burn books as though they're rubbish
And place a ban on anything published
After 1984?
(The novel, that is)
Is our best shot to overthrow the government
And replace it with our very own despot?
No

While our power structures may have produced the
problems
They are now no more than symptoms themselves
And their destruction
No answer
And the terrible explanation of this state is we're now at
war
With the very weapons we created to fight former wars;
That is to say
The methods we use to communicate and in which we all
collude
Are now the very means by which we're so confused.

So even as I wrote this
I knew there was only one solution
To stop writing and notice
To stop watching and see the system
To stop speaking and listen

Listen
Our tactics must be ingenious
We can't just switch off
Because our enemy's greatest skill

Is that to know his movements
We will be required
To stand still
And in the line of fire

Instead
Therefore
We must dare
To play the long game
And swear
That we will learn to be aware

Listen
To the infinitesimal silence
Between changing channels on your remote control
Hold onto that second before your alarm sounds
Ground yourself in the gaps in music
And the spaces between the words
And find truth in what you haven't heard
Instead of what you've heard

See
The cracks in the great tower
See
That power for all its abuse
Still requires our consent to be abused
See the terror on the faces of those in the highest places
And know they suffer vertigo

Notice
The capacity of our instincts
As distinct from our aspirations
As expressed in our fatally flawed
Communication.
Notice
That where language once defined our humanity
Now, through carelessness and vanity,
It was been refracted.

And where our thoughts could once be abstracted
In words,
Those words now signify only the ways we're distracted.

Listen. See. Notice

Notice the fear
Dare to stand in front of the mirror
And see how we're scared
This fear is to be owned
Now let us turn to our neighbours
See the fear in their eyes
Empathize and know we're not alone

Let us listen to what can no longer be said because of the
fatal damage we've inflicted on our language.

Notice. See. Listen

The tower of Babel is here
It stretches above us and pierces the sky
And we have to notice now
Or when it collapses we'll be left asking …

How?
What happened?
And, above all, why?